Baby Animals of the WORLD

Carmen Bredeson

CONTENTS

arctic (ARK tihk)—From the area around the North Pole.

blubber (BLUH bur)—Fat that has oil in it.

burrow (BUR oh)—A hole in the ground where animals live.

endangered (en DAYN jurd)—A type of animal that may disappear from Earth forever.

herds (hurdz)—Groups of plant-eating animals that live together.

pack (pak)—A group of meat-eating animals that live together.

poison (POY zun)—Something that can hurt or kill people and animals.

pouch (powch)—A bag used to hold something.

prey (pray)—An animal that is hunted and eaten for food.

tropical (TRAH pih kuhl)—In parts of the world that are warm and wet.

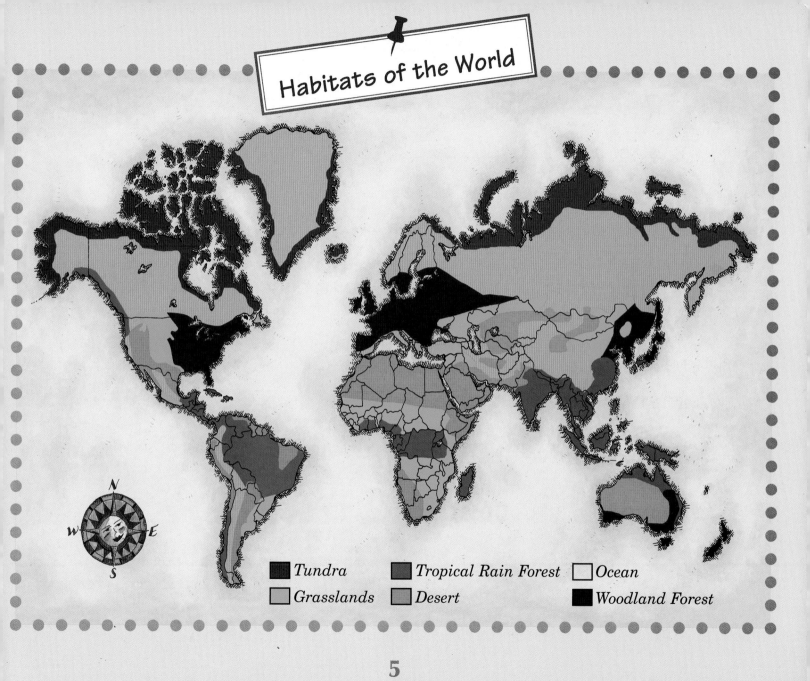

Habitats of the World

Tundra

Grasslands

Tropical Rain Forest

Desert

Ocean

Woodland Forest

TUNDRA

The tundra is very cold. Grasses and small plants grow, but there are no trees. The ground is frozen most of the year. The tundra is home to many animals. Baby animals have special ways to stay safe and live in the tundra.

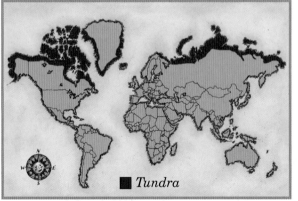

Tundra

BABY
ARCTIC FOX

Arctic fox pups are born in the spring. Their fur is brown like the grass. During the winter, the thick fur turns white. It helps them match the snow to stay safe from enemies. The foxes curl up in their bushy tails to stay warm.

A baby musk ox is called a calf. It crawls under its mother's long fur to keep warm. When danger is near, the adults make a circle around the calf. They point their sharp horns out to scare animals away.

BABY **MUSK OX**

BABY SNOWY OWL

Baby snowy owls hatch from eggs. Their parents bring food to the hungry chicks.

While the parents are away, the chicks stay VERY, VERY quiet. That is so wolves and foxes cannot find the chicks.

Wolves live in groups called **packs**. When cubs are born, the whole pack helps care for them. Wolves howl to each other. Sometimes the howl means danger is near.

Baby arctic wolves are called cubs.

BABY ARCTIC WOLF

BABY
DALL SHEEP

Dall lambs are born high up on a cliff. They stay safe from wolves and bears up there. As the lambs get bigger, their horns grow. The horns are made of the same thing as your fingernails.

Arctic tern chicks are very hungry. Their parents bring fish and insects for the chicks to eat. Arctic terns spend much of their time in the air. They fly from the North Pole to the South Pole and back EVERY year.

BABY **ARCTIC TERN**

A baby caribou is called a calf.

BABY **CARIBOU**

A caribou (KA rih boo) calf stands up just after it is born. Very soon the calf can walk. Caribou live in huge **herds**. They move from place to place eating grass. Calves must be able to move with the herd.

Tiny polar bear cubs tumble and play in the snow. Their fur is the same color as the snow. Today, the ice where the polar bears hunt is melting. It is getting harder and harder for the bears to find food.

ENDANGERED
ANIMAL OF THE
TUNDRA

BABY
POLAR BEAR

GRASSLANDS

Grasslands are covered with grasses.

There are not many trees or bushes.

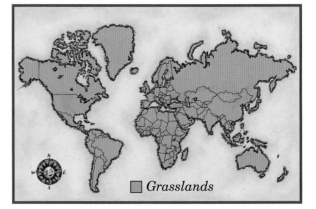

Grasslands

Animals have few places to hide.

Baby animals have special ways to stay safe and live in the grasslands.

BABY OSTRICH

Ostrich eggs are the biggest eggs in the world! The chicks hatch with feathers the color of dirt. This makes it easier to hide from enemies. An ostrich cannot fly, but it can run very, very FAST on its long legs.

Baby lions are called cubs. Their mother hides them in tall grass to keep them safe. Soon they will learn to hunt for **prey** like zebras and wild pigs. Lions see very well at night. That is when they usually look for food.

BABY LION

A baby bison is called a calf.

BABY **BISON**

A bison calf stays close to its mother. The calf has red hair when it is little. As the calf grows, its hair gets darker. Long, thick hair keeps the bison warm during the cold winter months.

A baby kangaroo is the size of a jelly bean when it is born. It is called a joey. The joey

drinks milk and grows in its mother's **pouch**. The joey's mother can hop very fast on her strong back legs.

BABY KANGAROO

BABY GIRAFFE

A baby giraffe is called a calf. It is as tall as a man. The calf can run a few hours after it is born. Giraffes are the tallest animals in the world.

Prairie dog pups are born in tunnels under the ground. After about six weeks, the pups crawl out of the tunnels. They hunt for insects and plants to eat. If danger is near, prairie dogs YIP, YIP, YIP to warn the others.

BABY
PRAIRIE DOG

BABY **BABOON**

A baby baboon rides on its mother's back as she looks for food. The baby learns which fruit and leaves are safe to eat. Baboons do not need to drink a lot of water. They get water from the food they eat.

A baby elephant stays close to its mother. It hides from danger under her legs. Big African elephants are sometimes killed by hunters. The hunters sell their tusks. Some elephants live in parks to stay safe from hunters.

ENDANGERED ANIMAL OF THE GRASSLANDS

BABY

AFRICAN ELEPHANT

TROPICAL RAIN FOREST

A lot of rain falls in warm **tropical** rain forests. Trees and plants grow very big. Many kinds of animal families live in rain forests. Baby animals have special ways to stay safe and live in the rain forest.

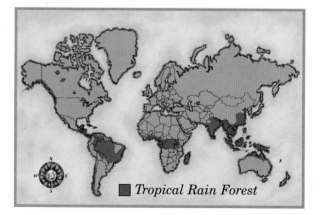

Tropical Rain Forest

BABY
CHIMPANZEE

The little chimp holds onto its mother. They swing from branch to branch. Up in the trees,

the chimps are safe from hunters. Their long arms reach for fruit and leaves to eat. Hold on tight, little chimp.

Frog tadpoles hatch from tiny eggs. Tadpoles start their lives in water. Then they turn into little frogs and hop onto land. These frogs have **poison** on their skin. The bright skin color tells other animals to STAY AWAY!

This mother frog carries a tadpole on her back.

BABY
POISON
DART FROG

BABY

HARPY EAGLE

A harpy eagle chick is white and fluffy. It hatches from an egg in a big nest. The nest is at the top of a tall tree. Both  mother and father take care of the chick. They bring it meat to eat.

Blue morphos are born as hairy little caterpillers. Then they turn into big blue butterflies. Their wings are brown on the bottom. When the butterfly folds its wings, it can hide in the brown branches.

BABY

BLUE MORPHO
BUTTERFLY

Baby jaguars are called cubs.

BABY JAGUAR

Jaguar cubs follow their mother and learn to hunt. Many jaguars live close to lakes or rivers in the rain forest. They are not like most cats. Jaguars like to SWIM! They catch fish to eat.

A baby elephant drinks milk from its mother. When it gets bigger, the baby eats leaves, grass, tree bark, and fruit. If there is danger, the baby runs to its mother. It scoots between her big legs to stay safe.

BABY
ASIAN
ELEPHANT

BABY SLOTH

A sloth spends its life hanging upside down from branches. A baby sloth hooks tiny claws into its mother's fur. They eat and sleep high up in the trees. Sloths move very, very slowly. They hide by looking like part of the tree.

Baby orangutans stay close
to their mothers. They live
high in the trees. There are few
orangutans left in the world.
The forests where they live have
been cut down. Many babies
have been stolen and sold as pets.

ENDANGERED
ANIMAL OF THE
RAIN FOREST

BABY
ORANGUTAN

DESERT

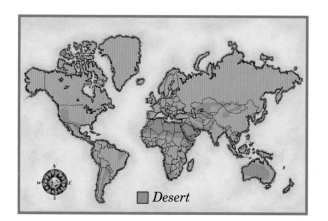

Desert

Deserts are very dry. Only a little bit of rain falls each year.

It can get very hot in the desert. Many desert animals hide from the sun during the day.

Baby animals have special ways to stay safe and live in the desert.

BABY **KIT FOX**

Baby kit foxes stay safe in a den when
they are little. Kit foxes have very BIG ears.
Big ears let out more heat from the fox's body
than little ears would. Big ears help keep
the foxes cool.

Sandgrouse babies are too little to go to a pond to drink. Their father can carry water in his belly feathers. He brings the water back to the nest. The thirsty chicks drink water right from the feathers.

Sandgrouse chicks can be hard to see!

BABY
SANDGROUSE

The big hump on a camel's back is made of fat. A camel uses the fat for energy when there is not much food to eat.

A baby camel does not have a big hump. It drinks milk from its mother. As the baby grows, so does the hump.

BABY MEERKAT

Baby meerkats are called pups. They are born in cool **burrows** under the ground. Their mothers bring mice and lizards to the burrow. The pups learn to hunt by chasing the little animals.

Baby burrowing owls do not live in a nest. They are born in a burrow. Their parents bring mice, beetles, and birds for the chicks to eat. The chicks learn to fly when they are only six weeks old.

BABY

BURROWING OWL

BABY GECKO

Geckos are a kind of lizard. Baby geckos hatch from eggs. Desert geckos hide from the hot sun under rocks and plants. They hunt for insects and spiders at night when it is cooler.

Bighorn lambs have tiny horn buds when they are born. As the lambs grow, so do their horns. There are not many bighorn sheep left in the world. Many have been killed for their beautiful horns.

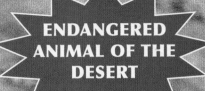
ENDANGERED ANIMAL OF THE DESERT

BABY
BIGHORN
SHEEP

OCEAN

Oceans cover much of the Earth. Some oceans are warm and some

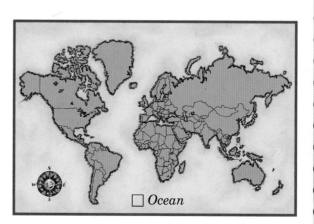

□ *Ocean*

oceans are cold. All oceans have salt water.

The ocean is home to many kinds of animals. Baby animals have special ways to stay safe and live in the ocean.

warm ocean   cold ocean

BABY HARP SEAL

Harp seal pups are born on the ice. Their fur is as white as snow. The pups learn to swim when they are only a few weeks old. Their thick fur and **blubber** keep them warm in the very cold water.

Baby dolphins make many sounds. They click, whistle, and squeak. That is how they talk to their mothers. Dolphins swim in groups. Swimming together is safer than swimming alone.

BABY

BOTTLENOSE DOLPHIN

BABY SEA OTTER

A sea otter pup rides on its mother's belly. She teaches her pup to swim and look for food. Sea otters find snails and crabs to eat. They use rocks to crack open the shells. Sea otters float on their backs while eating.

This baby turtle has a lot of growing to do!

Sea turtles lay eggs in the sand. The eggs hatch and the babies crawl to the ocean. They hide in seaweed and eat small crabs and shrimp.

BABY
SEA TURTLE

A little hermit crab finds a new home.

BABY
HERMIT CRAB

eggs

A hermit crab begins life in the ocean. It hatches from an egg and looks like a little fish. Soon it turns into a tiny crab and crawls onto the shore. The crab moves into a little seashell. As the crab grows, it moves to bigger and bigger shells.

anemone

eggs

The mother clown fish lays eggs under sea anemones. After the eggs hatch, the babies stay near the poisonous anemones. The anemone's sting does not hurt the clown fish. Other animals stay away from the anemone. The baby clown fish are safe.

Clown fish are also called anemonefish.

BABY
CLOWN FISH

BABY SEAHORSE

Baby seahorses grow inside eggs. Their father carries the eggs in a pouch on his belly. After the babies hatch, their father squirts them into the water. The babies hide in seaweed from hungry fish and crabs.

A father seahorse and his new babies.

Blue whales are the biggest animals on Earth. A blue whale pup is as long as a school bus when it is born. It stays close to its huge mother. There are not many blue whales left. They have been hunted for their blubber and for their meat.

ENDANGERED ANIMAL OF THE OCEAN

BABY
BLUE WHALE

WOODLAND FOREST

Woodland forests are full of trees, bushes, and rivers. The weather is cold in the winter and warm in the summer.

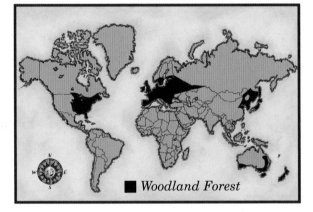

Woodland Forest

These forests are home to many kinds of animals. Baby animals have special ways to stay safe and live in the woodland forests.

95

BABY **OPOSSUM**

Baby opossums are tiny when they are born. They drink milk and grow in their mother's pouch. When they are bigger, the babies ride on their mother's back. She hunts for insects, nuts, and fruit for them to eat.

Black bear cubs are tiny when they are born in the winter. The cubs stay in a warm den with their mother. They drink their mother's milk and grow. When spring comes, the cubs leave the den for the first time.

BABY
BLACK BEAR

BABY
BALD EAGLE

A bald eagle chick hatches from an egg. Its parents bring the chick meat and fish to eat. The chick flaps its wings to make them strong. When it is about two months old, the little eagle flies for the first time.

Baby red foxes are born in a warm burrow. When they are bigger, their mother teaches them to hunt for mice, beetles, fruit, and frogs. Foxes have very furry tails. They use them like blankets when nights are cold.

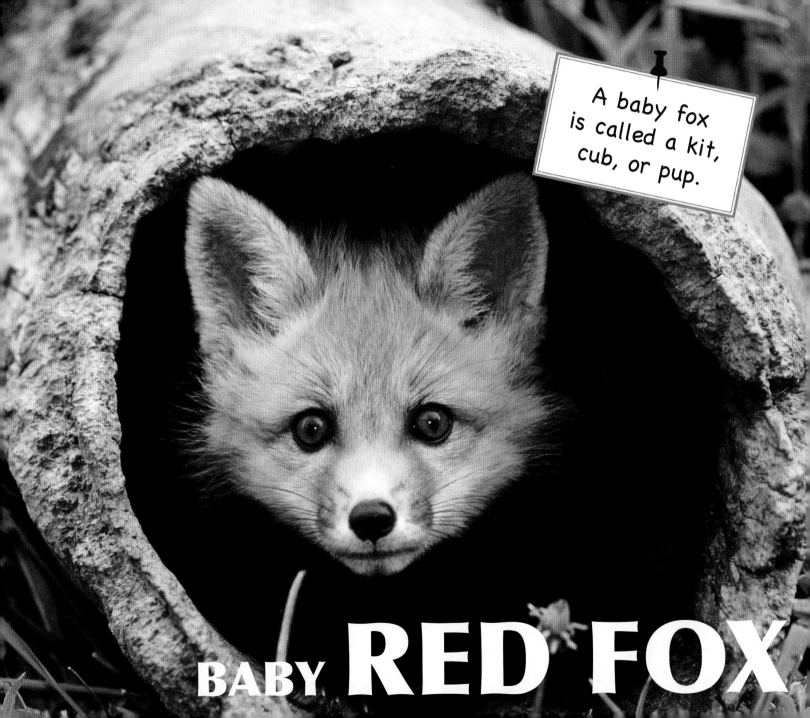

A baby fox is called a kit, cub, or pup.

BABY **RED FOX**

Five minutes old!

BABY **DEER**

A baby deer is called a fawn. It has spots on its fur for a few weeks. Spots help the fawn blend in with the plants and earth around it. This helps it stay safe from coyotes and wild dogs.

A baby hedgehog is born with pink skin. In a few hours, sharp spines start growing out of its back. To stay safe, the baby rolls into a ball with the spines sticking out.

BABY **HEDGEHOG**

A baby bobcat is called a kitten.

BABY **BOBCAT**

Bobcat kittens are born in a cave or hollow tree. After a few weeks, their mother brings live mice to her kittens. They practice hunting with the mice. Soon the kittens are ready to go on a real hunt for food.

A baby panda is TINY and pink. The cub's black and white fur starts to grow in about a month. There are not many pandas left in the world. They have been hunted for their fur. Their forest homes in China have been cut down.

ENDANGERED
ANIMAL OF
THE WOODLAND
FOREST

BABY
GIANT PANDA

Enslow Elementary, an imprint of Enslow Publishers, Inc.

Enslow Elementary® is a registered trademark of Enslow Publishers, Inc.

Library of Congress Cataloging-in-Publication Data

Bredeson, Carmen.
    Baby animals of the world / Carmen Bredeson.
        p. cm.
    Includes bibliographical references and index.
    Summary: "Up-close photos and information about baby animals in a variety of biomes"—Provided by publisher.
    ISBN 978-1-59845-218-1 (alk. paper)
    1. Animals—Infancy—Juvenile literature. 2. Habitat (Ecology)—Juvenile literature. I. Title.
    QL763.B64 2011
    591.3'9—dc22   2010030523

Printed in China

092010 Leo Paper Group, Heshan City, Guangdong, China

10 9 8 7 6 5 4 3 2 1

Note to Parents and Teachers: This book supports the National Science Education Standards for K–4 science. The Words to Know section introduces subject-specific vocabulary words, including pronunciation and definitions. Early readers may need help with these new words.

Series Science Consultant:
    Dennis L. Claussen, PhD
    Professor of Zoology
    Department of Zoology
    Miami University
    Oxford, OH

Series Literacy Consultant:
    Allan A. De Fina, PhD
    Dean, College of Education/Department of Literacy Education
    New Jersey City University
    Jersey City, NJ
    Past President of the New Jersey Reading Association

Photo Credits: Alamy: © Keren Su/China Span, pp. 110, 111, © Manor Photography, p. 36, © Mark Conlin, p. 84; **Alaskastock:** © 2010 Ken Baehr, p. 100, © 2010 Judy Holmes, p. 78, © 2010 Patrick Endres, p. 21, © 2010 Ronald S. Phillips, p. 17, © 2010 Steven Kazlowski, p. 10; **Animals Animals:** © Barbara Von Hoffmann, p. 41, © D. Allen Photography, p. 39, © D&J Bartlett/OSF, p. 27, © Dominique Braud, p. 101, © Erwin & Peggy Bauer, pp. 37, 108, © Gordon & Cathy Illg, p. 97, © Ingrid Van Den Berg, p. 26, © S. Michael Bisceglie, p. 30; **Arcticphoto.com:** © Wayne Lynch, p. 11; © **1999 Artville, LLC,** pp. 5, 6, 24, 42, 60, 76, 94; **ardea.com:** © Francois Gohier, p. 93, © Nick Gordon p. 53, © Thomas Dressler, p. 69, © Tom & Pat Leeson, p. 82; © **Charlie Phillips/SpecialistStock,** p. 81; **Corbis:** © Darrell Gulen, p. 8, © Jenny E. Ross, p. 23, © Michael & Patricia Fogden, p. 65; © **Frans Lanting/www.lanting.com,** pp. 59, 83; **Getty Images:** © George Grall, pp. 46, 90, © Michael S. Quinton, p. 18, © Scott T. Smith, p. 62, © Sean Russell, p. 74; **iStockphoto.com:** © Dmitry Deshevykh, p. 2 (left), © Les Cunliffe, p. 43, © saints4757, p. 40, © Sebastien Cote, p. 50 (left); **Minden Pictures:** © Anup Shah/npl, p. 44, © Bruce Davidson/npl, p. 72, © Chris Newbert, p. 89, © Cyril Ruoso/JH Editorial, p. 45, © Gerry Ellis, pp. 66, 103, © Jim Brandenburg, pp. 14, 15, © Michael & Patricia Fogden, pp. 47, 56, 57, © Michio Hoshino, pp. 12, 79, © Mitsuaki Iwago, p. 28, © Patricio Robles Gil, p. 20, © Pete Oxford, p. 54, © Paul Hobson/FLPA, p. 107, © Richard Du Toit, p. 35, © S & D & K Maslowski, p. 98, © SA Team/Foto Natura, p. 52, © Suzi Eszterhas, pp. 31, 99, © Tui De Roy, p. 49, © Winfried Wisniewski, p. 13, © Yva Momatiuk & John Eastcott, pp. 9 (left), 34, 61, © ZSSD, p. 75; **naturepl.com:** © Anup Shah, pp. 55, 58, © Dave Watts, p. 32, © Doug Perrine, pp. 85, 91, © Eric Baccega, p. 22, © Jane Burton, pp. 86, 106, © Jeff Rotman, p. 80, © John Cancalosi, p. 63, © Konstantin Mikhailov, p. 19, © Michael D. Kern, p. 50 (right), © Pete Oxford, pp. 33, 48, © Philippe Clement, p. 7, © Suzi Eszterhas, p. 29, © T. J. Rich, p. 102, © Tom Vezo, p. 70; **Photoshot:** © Bruce Coleman, p. 67, © Oceans-Image, p. 73, © NHPA, pp. 9 (right), 16, 64, 68, 87; © **Phillip Colla/Oceanlight.com,** p. 92; **Photo Researchers, Inc.:** © ArtWolfe, p. 109, © David Hall, p. 88, © Stuart Wilson, p. 51; **Shutterstock.com,** pp. 2 (middle, right), 3, 25, 38, 71, 77, 95, 96, 104, 105.

Front Cover Photos: © Judy Holmes/AlaskaStock.com (top right), © Doug Perrine/naturepl.com (bottom middle), © Paul Hobson/FLPA/Minden Pictures (top left); © Peter Blackwell/naturepl.com (top middle); © SA Team/Foto Natura/Minden Pictures (bottom left), Shutterstock.com (bottom right).

Back Cover Photos: Shutterstock.com

Enslow Elementary
an imprint of
Enslow Publishers, Inc.

E 40 Industrial Road
Box 398
Berkeley Heights, NJ 07922
USA

http://www.enslow.com